UNIVERSITY OF MINNESOTA

P9-DFR-957

The American Short Story

BY DANFORTH ROSS

UNIVERSITY OF MINNESOTA PRESS · MINNEAPOLIS

© Copyright 1961 by the University of Minnesota

ALL RIGHTS RESERVED

Printed in the United States of America at the North Central
Publishing Company, St. Paul

Library of Congress Catalog Card Number: 61-63843

PUBLISHED IN GREAT BRITAIN, INDIA, AND PAKISTAN BY THE OXFORD
UNIVERSITY PRESS, LONDON, BOMBAY, AND KARACHI, AND IN
CANADA BY THOMAS ALLEN, LTD., TORONTO

THE AMERICAN SHORT STORY

DANFORTH ROSS teaches courses in short story writing
and modern literature at Southwestern at Memphis.
He has taught previously at the University of
Minnesota and at Columbia University.

⌁ The American Short Story

Whatever its universal qualities, the good literature of every nation expresses the national character. This is as true of American literature as of any other. However, in the beginning American literature tended to express a hybrid European character, not surprisingly, for American writers were after all primarily a product of European influences. Their problem lay in finding a way to express American character while at the same time remaining true to their European heritage. Since this was largely an unrecognized problem, they solved it slowly, inadvertently, ironically, without realizing what they were up to. By so doing, they achieved a literature with unmistakable European roots yet with a tone its own. This can be seen with special clarity in the literary form that is known as the short story.

Although short stories of one sort or another had been part of literature from its earliest expressions, writers were just beginning to theorize about the possibilities of the short story at the start of the nineteenth century. The first important American short story writer, Washington Irving (1783–1859), was something of a theorist himself. Irving believed in a relaxed kind of story, what he called a sketch. "I consider a story merely as a frame on which to sketch my materials." If we measure Irving's ideas against Aristotle's *Poetics*, the work most often drawn upon in theorizing about fiction as well as about drama, we see that he put less emphasis on action and theme than did Aristotle, more on character. He aimed at "the weaving in of character, lightly yet expressively delineated." Possibly influenced by an eighteenth-century writer like Addison, he also thought of his story as a vehicle to express local color and to reveal his own personality, objectives that Aristotle would scarcely have approved. He valued "the familiar and faithful exhibition of scenes of common life; and the half-concealed vein of humor that is often playing through the whole."

This is the theoretical Irving. The actual Irving often wrote stories that were deficient in character, in scenes close to common life, and in humor. He wrote at a time when many European writers sought the faraway and the exotic, or presented the closeby as if it were faraway. Their quasi-Romantic influence shows up in some of Irving's stories — in *The Alhambra* tales, for example. These stories are too imitative of their European models, too cut off from life. The action is contrived and melodramatic, the character delineation shallow, the dialogue archaic.

It was primarily in his American stories or sketches that Irving followed his theory. And here we find him at his best. In several of these stories, notably "Rip Van Winkle" and "The Legend of Sleepy Hollow," he achieves something unexpected, representation of the national character. I say unexpected, because in both these stories Irving goes to German legends for his ideas. Yet instead of presenting German stories in American dress, he adapts the legends to the American scene and comes up with characters who are unmistakably American.

Both Rip Van Winkle and Ichabod Crane are made so individual that we can almost touch them, so general that they have become a part of our national heritage. Rip is an exaggerated portrayal of the henpecked husband. He is the forerunner of that twentieth-century creation of James Thurber, Walter Mitty, but more rugged than Mitty. Ichabod is an equally universal character — the American schoolmaster up to the end of the nineteenth century and beyond. Never sure of his place in the community or of himself, he is held in mingled respect and ridicule and is the butt of practical jokes. Irving treats him with sympathy and humor and no sentimentality. Brom Bones, the man who gets the best of Ichabod, is also an authentic American character. He is not exactly the frontiersman, but he has some of the characteristics of the frontiersman — masculinity, anti-intellectualism, and a broad humor that relies on the practical joke and the tall tale. He is the man who has reduced the stature of the American schoolteacher, made him a figure to be humorously tolerated but never completely accepted.

The action of both stories is episodic and slowed by expository and descriptive passages that sometimes are not functional. In keeping with his conception of the short story, Irving is relaxed, not in a hurry. He mediates between his materials and the reader. But his humor makes him a delightful mediator. And he does eventually pull things together. The stories do move toward climaxes. The action also has psychological validity — even Rip's experience with the men playing at ninepins in the Catskills and his long sleep. It is significant that Rip does not return home till the day after his shrewish wife dies. He has succeeded in escaping her, just as Walter Mitty has his way of going off into fantasy to escape Mrs. Mitty. However, the amnesia is not insisted on; it is simply implicit in the story.

Coleridge once said that the Gothic horror motif had palled on him. He "was wearied with fiends, incomprehensible characters, with shrieks, murders, and subterranean dungeons." But in "The Legend of Sleepy Hollow" Irving makes use of the Gothic devices without being victimized by them. As with Rip's twenty-year sleep, he brings them into the context of American life and humanizes them with his humor. He plays upon Ichabod's susceptibility to Gothic horror, upon his willingness to believe in the existence of a headless horseman.

Irving does not seem to have any very serious intent in either

7

story. He wants to exhibit the "scenes of common life" and to let his "half-concealed vein of humor" play over the whole. Yet the effect is satirical. However sympathetically, he is exposing foibles in American life and character.

One further point about Irving: Though his description is somewhat diffusely presented, he has an excellent pictorial sense. He sees with the painter's eye. One is not surprised to learn that he at one time considered making a career of painting. Irving's scenic effects seem to be soft, somewhat atmospheric, like those of the Hudson River School, yet with a humorous tone absent from the works of painters of this school.

Edgar Allan Poe (1809–1849), more of a theorizer than Irving, is in accord with Aristotle as far as he goes. In fact, Poe brings *The Poetics* to the short story and becomes the first American to visualize the story as an art form. Like Aristotle, he makes character subsidiary to action. And like Aristotle, he sees each element of the story as subsidiary to the action as a whole. The "literary artist," Poe says, conceives "a certain unique or single *effect* to be wrought out" and "then invents such incidents" and "combines such events as may best aid him in establishing this preconceived effect. . . . In the whole composition there should be no word written, of which the tendency, direct or indirect, is not to the one pre-established design. And by such means, with such care and skill, a picture is at length painted which leaves in the mind of him who contemplates it with a kindred art, a sense of the fullest satisfaction."

This theory announces the modern story. When followed, it brings for the first time tension, long a characteristic of poetry, to the story. Irving's stories meander along, Poe's are compressed and tight. Then too, the writer obeying the precepts of this theory presents his story, as a dramatist presents a scene in a play, rather than explains or narrates or relates the action. When Irving presents, it is almost by accident; with Poe, presenting is habitual and the result of conscious effort. There will also not be overpainted parts of the canvas, and other parts that are bare of detail. Poe's stories have a sharpness of shape, of form, that Irving's lack. Finally the theory means that the reader is pulled toward one single moment, the moment of effect, in which he has "a sense of the fullest satisfaction."

It is in the effects he is after that Poe falls short of Aristotle. Effects for Aristotle have the function of revealing universal truth or, as he puts it, "thought." Thought to Poe is simply means to effect. For example, he leans upon the Romantic movement in "Ligeia," with the purpose not of dramatizing its ideas but of enhancing the effect of Gothic horror he is after.

Place is also a means to effect with Poe, and as a result it is not so crucial in his stories as in Irving's. Whereas Irving goes wrong when he chooses a foreign setting, Poe ranges far and wide and is always at home with his materials. He chooses his locale in relationship to the effect that he is after and then develops only those characteristics of the locale that will contribute to the effect. Thus he is not interested in place in itself.

Poe wrote four kinds of stories: mystery or detective; science fiction; Gothic horror stories that emphasize atmospherics and the supernatural; and Gothic horror stories that emphasize action. The mystery or detective stories ("The Purloined Letter," "The Murders in the Rue Morgue," etc.) are masterpieces in a minor vein, a vein largely invented by Poe. In M. Dupin, Poe portrayed the prototype for Sherlock Holmes. These stories are called "tales of ratiocination" because of Poe's meticulous attention to the rational process by which mysteries are unraveled. His science fiction stories ("The Gold Bug," for example) are developed with the same careful regard for rational credibility.

Stories like "Ligeia" and "The Fall of the House of Usher" run afoul of Coleridge's weariness "with fiends" and "incomprehen-

9

sible characters." The modern reader, with his scientific suspicion of the supernatural, finds it hard to suspend the will to disbelieve. In relying upon Gothic and Romantic conventions, Poe loses contact with psychological validity. It is true that hidden sins are hinted at in both stories, but the reader can never clearly grasp them or the vague motivations of the characters. He finds no clue to the social context in which the Usher family suffers its fall. He refuses to accept Ligeia's supernatural reappearance as the result of the Romantic vigor with which she projects her will. The terror of Poe's effects do not cut into the marrow of his being.

It is a different matter with Poe's action horror stories. Even those that do no more than create suspense ("The Pit and the Pendulum," "The Descent into the Maelstrom," etc.) are as good at this level as the mystery stories. A few, however, are more concerned with subjective action than with what happens on the surface. These do what is only vaguely hinted at in "Ligeia" and "The Fall of the House of Usher" — they reveal the diseased surface of life to rise from a diseased undersurface. They deal with the problem of evil.

In "The Black Cat" a man happily adjusted to wife and pets takes to drink and gradually becomes irritable and moody. He is beset with a compulsion to hurt what he has previously loved, and one day he turns on his favorite pet, a black cat, and cuts out one eye. He immediately reacts with feelings of guilt, but they are "feeble and equivocal . . . and the soul remained untouched." He plunges again into excess, and, led on by an "unfathomable longing of the soul *to vex itself*," hangs the cat. Eventually he acquires another black cat, which, because it reminds him of the first cat, he comes to dread. One day, exasperated to madness, he strikes at the animal with an ax and, when his wife stops the blow, turns on her and buries the ax in her brain. He then walls up her body in the cellar. The police eventually come, and, though they can find nothing amiss in the cellar, he cannot resist the compulsion to talk and even to rap his cane on the brickwork. At this the cat, accidentally entombed with the wife, wails out, and the gory crime is exposed.

Perhaps in this story Poe is probing his own disturbed inner state. In any event, the reader experiences the state of mind of the guilty man, because he recognizes impulses that he himself has but tends to keep hidden, especially the impulse to kill what he most loves, the impulse to do violence to his own nature. Thus the terror for the reader is not the pleasurable terror of Gothic horror. Nor is it Aristotle's terror mingled with a pity that brings a sense of catharsis. It is a neurotic's terror. The reader comes away from the story, as from Strindberg's *Miss Julie*, with nerves laid raw.

Nathaniel Hawthorne (1804–1864) was the first American writer of the short story to concern himself seriously with theme. Whereas Poe and Irving only occasionally, and then inadvertently, brought out Aristotle's element of thought in their stories, Hawthorne went to the opposite extreme. However, he lacked Poe's concern for effect, and he had a tendency to teach his moral point rather than to dramatize it. Instead of implying his point and thereby setting up reverberations in us, he *tells* us what we are to believe.

In developing his themes, mostly centered around the problem of good and evil, Hawthorne relied upon allegory and what he called romance. His allegorical tales are often heavily didactic. In "The Great Stone Face" Ernest spends his life looking for a man with exactly such a face as the gigantic one sculptured by nature in the mountains near his home. The people of Ernest's community, absorbed in worldly pursuits, mistakenly see in the big men of America images of the Great Stone Face. But Ernest, with his eyes always on the Face itself (on God), is able to see the falsity of these images. At the end we discover it is Ernest himself who resembles the Face. The story becomes a warning against the vanity of self-seeking and tells us to turn our thoughts heavenward. However, Hawthorne is so didactic in his allegorical presentation that he denies us the aesthetic pleasure of discovering the theme ourselves. The setting is vaguely New England, but we never have the feeling that the characters are less allegorical than their names. Nor does the action have tension.

A more successful allegorical story is "The Celestial Omnibus." Here good-natured satire replaces the heavy seriousness of "The Great Stone Face." The story is *Pilgrim's Progress* in reverse. Christian takes the hard road to heaven, but these journeyers, living in a nineteenth-century America in which sin has disappeared, go by train and enjoy themselves along the way. Again the vanity of human wishes is attacked, but the reader comes away from the story delighted at the insight he has gained.

Hawthorne's idea of romance, as he explained in the Preface to *The House of the Seven Gables*, was to take material true to the human heart and cast over it an "evanescent flavor" of the "Marvelous." He added that the writer should not get too far away from ordinary reality but that he did not commit a literary crime even if he did. This concept of romance, which has something of the Gothic in it, led Hawthorne to be suspicious of America as a setting for his stories and novels. In the Preface to *The Marble Faun* he pointed to "the difficulty of writing a romance about a country where there is no shadow, no antiquity, no mystery, no picturesque and gloomy wrong . . ."

It is not surprising then that in seeking a setting in which to give his romances root Hawthorne sometimes looked to Europe. But these are not his most successful works. "Rappacini's Daughter," laid in Italy and peopled by Italians, is about a man so dedicated to science that he conducts an experiment in which he violates the sanctity of the human heart — he sacrifices his daughter to his insatiable quest for knowledge. Hawthorne has a good theme: he is attacking the overemphasis on reason during the Enlightenment, showing the consequences of subordinating other human values to the rational. But in developing his exotic Italian setting and in overlaying it with the supernatural (the mere touch of a flower in Rappacini's garden or of his daughter will poison a person physically and morally), Hawthorne has got so far away from reality that he loses his modern reader.

Despite the absence of antiquity in America, his native land comes off better in Hawthorne's stories than does Europe. In the New England past and in the American wilderness, Hawthorne did find settings congenial to his idea of romance. Some of these stories ("Ethan Brand," "The Birth-Mark") have the same didactic quality and overplayed Gothic horror found in "Rappacini's Daughter." But others ("Young Goodman Brown," "Roger Malvin's Burial," "The Artist of the Beautiful") are more realistic and more connotative in their presentation. This is particularly true of "Young Goodman Brown." The story is laid in seventeenth-century Salem and dramatizes the dilemma of Brown, who brings his Puritan repressions into his marriage with a refreshingly innocent and spontaneous girl named Faith. Uncomfortable with her and her pink ribbons, Brown seeks outlet in a Witch's Sabbath and discovers repressed impulses not only in himself but in other Puritans. Instead of emerging from this "heart of darkness" with compassion for the weaknesses of man, he takes pride in repressing anew and turns a grim face toward the other citizens of Salem, feeling his own superiority. The climactic moment of the story comes when he looks "sternly and sadly" into Faith's face and passes her "without a greeting." The reader experiences with horror what it means to be a particular kind of Puritan.

The theme, it will be noted, is a variation of that found in the other stories commented on here — man's failure through pride and his need for humility and compassion. Despite didactic passages, especially at the end, Hawthorne reveals his theme in "Young Goodman Brown" dramatically, so that it strikes the reader with the force of shock. The opening scene when Brown comes forth from Salem village, the symbolic treatment of Faith's pink ribbons, and the confrontation of Faith by Brown after his return to the village — all testify to Hawthorne's dramatic effectiveness. So does the handling of the element of Gothic romance in Brown's midnight encounter with Satan and in the lurid cavortings of the townspeople in the forest. These are more than Gothic trappings: they are the nightmare projections of Brown's mind. Thus the Gothic motif need not be taken literally but is seen in ambiguity, setting up reverberations in the reader's consciousness.

In the better stories by Hawthorne the reader becomes aware of the New England character. In those of Herman Melville (1819–1891) he discovers American character. Perhaps Melville's New York background is partly responsible. New York as the heart of a buffer region between New England and the South developed a more composite life than they did. Melville also dramatizes the nineteenth-century present, which is more broadly American than the Puritan past.

Like Hawthorne, Melville is concerned with the problem of good and evil. In "The Tartarus of Maids" he poses this problem in the context of the Industrial Revolution. He seems to anticipate the naturalist writers in showing the girls who work in a New England paper mill to be victims of mechanization. Pale, lifeless, they are not even permitted to marry, because the organic pattern of childbirth would interfere with the machine pattern of the paper mill. But Melville goes beyond the naturalists in that, instead of stressing the need for a more beneficent industrial system, he broods upon man's willingness to permit his fellow human beings to be dehumanized. As dramatized by the boy Cupid, who

14

is callously indifferent to the fate of the girls, the root of the problem becomes man's innate evil.

No more than Hawthorne does Melville put first emphasis on technique. However, in stubbornly wrestling with great materials he sometimes achieves or nearly achieves startling technical successes. In *The Poetics* Aristotle speaks of recognition and irony as central elements in the development of tragic action. Oedipus, for example, eventually recognizes himself as the defiler of Thebes. In the greatest tragedy recognition is combined with irony. Thus the recognition by Oedipus comes with surprise; it is the opposite of that expected.

In "Bartleby, the Scrivener" Melville is working very subtly (perhaps unconsciously) with irony. We start off thinking that Bartleby is the crucial character; gradually we learn that the Wall Street lawyer who tells the story is really presenting his own crisis, not Bartleby's. It centers around the scriveners in his office, men engaged in copying legal documents, work as boring and dehumanizing as that of tending machinery in a paper mill. Seeking only security and pleasure from life, the lawyer would have them become automatons. Two of them circumvent him by reserving half of each working day for neurotic eccentricity, thus salvaging their humanity, though at the cost of neuroticism. The third scrivener, Bartleby, is the perfect robot when he works, but refuses to carry out certain orders of the lawyer. "I would prefer not to," he says again and again. Finally he refuses to work altogether, or even to leave the premises. Both lawyer and reader are greatly upset by Bartleby's behavior, apparently because, though the lawyer never fully understands this, what Bartleby is refusing to serve are the false gods of a dehumanized world. Through his negation, ending finally in death, Bartleby has sacrificed himself for higher values. Nor has his sacrifice been completely in vain, for the complacency of the lawyer has been at least temporarily shaken. And this is the point of irony, the unexpected discovery by the lawyer of his own hollowness. He has been made gropingly aware that he is spiritually dead himself, that he stares out at the same blank walls that confront Bartleby, that he must choose between his own no-life and spiritual life. And yet his no-life is so much the life of the enveloping community that the choice is not really clear to him. He can only cry, "Ah Bartleby! Ah humanity!" He is a hollow man with partial insight, not Conrad's Kurtz, not Tolstoy's Ivan Ilyich. But like them, he has been made existentially aware of the need for choice.

Thus Melville's story is as American as Wall Street, but has significance for the whole modern world.

As Americans pushed farther and farther west, returning again and again to primitive conditions, the frontier began to have an effect on the American short story. To begin with, this influence was completely nonprofessional. It appeared in absurd, technically crude stories that exaggerated the individualistic feats of westerners. These "tall tales" expressed the spirit of the West, the zest and the defensive assertiveness, and they were told in the vernacular, the language of the audience. They owed nothing to Aristotle, or to the Romantic movement, or to the Gothic horror tradition, or to any other historical influence except perhaps that of democratic individualism. Their authors were anonymous.

Eventually the professionals took over the tall tales, at first gropingly, and then more and more subtly and pervasively, until today it is hard to tell exactly how our important contemporary writers reflect the frontier and yet we feel that many of them do. In writers of a hundred years ago the influence is easy to see. They showed an increasing tendency to use American settings and a vernacular language and a broad rough humor. They used a looser form and looser technique than did Poe and Hawthorne. Basically they were more concerned with subject matter than form. They still reflected European influences, but a more American flavor had crept in.

The tall tales were first given professional treatment by eastern writers like Augustus Longstreet who showed easterners trying to come to terms with the West. The point of view and language are those of the East. Then, as in "The Big Bear of Arkansas," by T. B. Thorpe, an eastern narrator meets a westerner who tells a story in his own language. (This particular story, about a bear that can't be hunted down, provides the germinal idea for Faulkner's great story, "The Bear.") Finally George W. Harris discards the eastern narrator and lets the western story, with its vigor of language and event, come through with full force. Harris's hero is a Jacksonian individualist who ridicules learning and gentility.

Samuel Langhorne Clemens (1835–1910), a westerner by birth, struck the keynote for the vernacular language when he chose as his pen name "Mark Twain." This name, springing spontaneously from his river-boating experience, makes the real name "Clemens" fall upon our ears with a false ring.

Some of Twain's best stories are in the tradition of the frontier tall tale in both subject matter and language. In "The Celebrated Jumping Frog of Calaveras County" Twain starts off with an eastern narrator, who introduces the real narrator, a westerner. Speaking in the vernacular, the westerner relates the tall tale of still another westerner, a wildly aggressive gambler. The gambler is a caricature and the incidents bring out nothing momentous, but Twain's ear for the language of his westerners is perfect and the story is wonderfully funny.

Twain's troubles come when he tries to wed western and eastern influences. He is too much of an individualistic westerner to give serious attention to the problem of form, too respectful of eastern culture to trust the western language he used so well. "The Man

17

That Corrupted Hadleyburg" is similar to "Young Goodman Brown" in that Twain is exposing a deep moral flaw in the American community. The people of Hadleyburg, a midwestern town, are so shielded from temptation that they take pride in their morality and are hard, mean people. But unlike Hawthorne, Twain fails to dramatize his theme successfully. For one thing, the handling of point of view is too loose. He lacks a character, like Goodman Brown, to let the action come through. As a result the story fails in form. It sprawls. Finally the story fails in language. The language is that of Samuel Clemens, a kind of purified western. It is not bad in itself, but lacks a sense of feel for the occasion. It is hybrid.

In Bret Harte (1836–1902), an easterner who moved to California at nineteen and wrote stories about the West, chiefly about the Gold Rush period, literary virtues and shortcomings are so mixed that it is hard to evaluate him fairly. One finds in his work an amazing simplicity and boldness and freshness and humor. He seems to cut through hampering restrictions and to breathe fresh air. But he isn't able to carry through to the end and his oversimplified dramatic solutions mark the literary hack rather than the serious artist.

Harte writes about rough happenings in mining towns, about gamblers and prostitutes and violent death. As Henry Adams points out in his *Education*, he is one of the few writers of his time bold enough to treat sex other than sentimentally, at least in so far as his audience will permit him. But his characters are stereotypes and the actions in which they figure are sketched rather than carefully worked out. His characters are also sentimentalized. Oakhurst, the tough gambler in "The Outcasts of Poker Flat," may have a heart of gold, but Harte seems more intent on asserting the irony than in demonstrating it. Even Harte's relaxed, vigorous language is marred by sentimentality. Influenced by his reading rather than by his observation, he falls into clichés. For example, in "The Luck of Roaring Camp" nature stops to listen when a baby is born. "The pines stopped moaning, the river ceased to rush, and the fire to crackle." Here Harte fails through being insufficiently western.

A greater master of the story form is Ambrose Bierce (1842–1914?), a literary son of Poe. Every word, every detail, every incident in his stories works toward the effect he is attempting to achieve. He is also like Poe in that he makes use of Gothic horror, but with less resort to the supernatural. In an age increasingly influenced by science, he had to root horror in reality. A still further likeness to Poe is that Bierce's stories are limited in thematic scope and complexity of character development. It is the shock effect he is after, no deep insight into man's nature. However, his shocks are genuinely unnerving, in contrast to the shallow and obvious ones of a writer like O. Henry.

Bierce is best known for his Civil War stories, but he also makes dramatic use of the frontier. In "The Boarded Window" the isolation and loneliness of life on the frontier have set up a state of mind in a man that makes it possible for him to believe that his sick wife is dead. Hence, when we learn at the end of the story that she has been killed by a panther while he sits beside her in a dazed sleep, our experience of shock is not dissipated by any feeling that Bierce has tricked us with supernatural hocus-pocus. The shock is felt far more than that in "The Fall of the House of Usher" or "Ligeia" and prepares the way for Faulkner's "A Rose for Emily."

"An Occurrence at Owl Creek Bridge," the best known of the Civil War stories, is interesting technically in that Bierce achieves his horror effect by dramatizing a major portion of the action through the consciousness of a man hovering between life and death. He gives a third-person presentation of Peyton Farquhar standing upon a bridge, waiting to be hung, then plunges into Farquhar's consciousness. Writing before the discovery of the irrational stream of consciousness by psychologists, Bierce presents Farquhar's inner experience in a rational flow but with great intensity.

At the same time that the frontier influence was invigorating American writing and loosening it up, a counter influence was emasculating it. The Genteel Tradition, with its emphasis upon ideals sheltered from testing in what Conrad has called the "sea of experience," lifted the writer into a rarefied atmosphere. This influence was especially destructive to minor talents like Thomas Bailey Aldrich ("Marjorie Daw"), but it also hampered more virile writers like Twain and Harte. Occasionally writers did resist the Genteel Tradition by examining it in their stories, by making it the subject matter for drama. Among those freeing themselves to a limited extent was William Dean Howells (1837–1920), who, with Twain and Henry James, assumed leadership in American fiction during the last quarter of the nineteenth century. In "Editha," for example, he implies that patriotism cut off from knowledge of life is a dangerous thing. In this story Editha threatens to break with her fiancé because he hesitates to fight in a war that she believes in. She tells him that "God meant it to be war" and refuses to see him again unless he volunteers. He gives in and is killed. She then turns the whole thing to her advantage, regarding herself as one who has nobly sacrificed; she lacks the compassion to suffer for the man or for his mother. At the end she sees the upset mother as vulgar and takes pride in having her own ideal beauty glorified by a genteel painter.

Though the story is told partly through the eyes of Editha, the reader is continually above her, discovering her shortcomings and those of people like her. Howells achieves his satirical effect more successfully than Twain in "The Man That Corrupted Hadleyburg." The reason lies in his more careful ordering of materials. Technically he is working in the tradition of Poe, pushing toward a single effect.

Whereas Howells only partly escaped the Genteel Tradition, Henry James (1843–1916) made it a major subject for analysis and overcame it "in the classic way," as Santayana has pointed out, "by understanding it." He also made a thorough study of technique and ranks with Poe in his contributions to it. Actually his pursuit of technique led to his understanding of the Genteel Tradition.

What James did in a sense was simply to reinterpret Aristotle's conception of recognition in the light of modern psychological studies of subjective experience. His primary concern was to direct what his brother, psychologist William James, called a "stream of thought" toward a moment of recognition. It was always a controlled, rational stream, however. He simply worked with the conscious interior experience of his central character, seeking to highlight moments of illumination. He often theorized to this effect, as, for example, in the Preface to *The American*, when he said of Christopher Newman, "the interest of everything is all that it is *his* vision, *his* conception, *his* interpretation."

This approach to fiction looks back to romanticism in that it views life from a subjective center, but it does so without the Romantic's mystic expectations. It is actually closer to impressionism, since the central character is at all times seeking an impression of some aspect of the world around him. In any event, it is through shocks of recognition that James's stories get their movement.

Often in James's stories the character seeking illumination is genteel — hence caught in a conflict between his desire for experience and the inhibitions of gentility. Some of James's characters win the struggle, others run from life. The most celebrated character who runs is John Marcher, in "The Beast in the Jungle."

Marcher makes a cult of seeking experience, yet avoids it. Finally he recognizes his failure to face experience as itself a terrible kind of experience. He has run right into the path of "the beast in the jungle."

At times in James the genteel character is an object for examination by the character who is seeking illumination. In "The Real Thing" a genteel couple, Major and Mrs. Monarch, persuade an artist to use them as models. They argue that since they are the "real thing," representatives of gentility, he will be saved the labor of creating them. But he discovers that the "real thing" for him is the imaginative experience of creation, that Major and Mrs. Monarch are, with the best of good will, trying to emasculate him, to cut him off from life, to reduce him to their own aridity. Nevertheless, he values the experience of having worked with them, of having gained insight into them and into himself. Hence in the artist we have a triumphant Jamesian character; in a sense, James himself.

An early disciple of James, Edith Wharton (1862–1937) carefully ordered her materials toward the illumination she wanted her reader to receive. Often her intention was at least partly satirical; upper middle-class people living narrow decorous lives are made fun of as they seek to give their lives meaning without essentially changing them. No more than James does she defend these lives.

In "The Mission of Jane" Miss Wharton exposes an unsuccessful marriage. The story for the most part is oriented through the husband, who feels that he is more perceptive than his dull wife. He tries to make the best of their arid marriage by "taking refuge in the somewhat rarefied atmosphere of his perceptions," but the wife is determined that they shall not lead separate lives and seeks to bring him back into the fold by adopting a child. Unfortunately Jane proves to be even duller than the wife, and she achieves her mission in an ironic way. She draws Lethbury and his wife together, not by fulfilling Mrs. Lethbury's romantic expectations of what parenthood should mean, but through the ordeal that parenthood sometimes actually entails, that of getting an unattractive daughter married. Miss Wharton achieves her dramatic reversal deftly. She also reveals an ability to look at life as it is, not as she might want it to be. She refuses to sentimentalize marriage or parenthood.

Another story exposing the aridity of the Genteel Tradition is "A New England Nun," by Mary E. Wilkins Freeman (1852–1930). The "nun" of the story, Louisa Ellis, lives such a sheltered life that when marriage looms she runs from the roughness of her fiancé. "Louisa's feet had turned into a path, smooth maybe under a calm, serene sky, but so straight and unswerving that it could only meet a check at her grave, and so narrow that there was no room for anyone at her side." Still, if she "had sold her birthright she did not know it, the taste of the pottage was so delicious, and had been her sole satisfaction for so long."

Sarah Orne Jewett (1849–1909) also writes stories about New England, but with the intent of evoking local color. Unlike Mrs. Freeman, she does not look for the universal in the human condition as revealed in the context of New England life, but seeks to bring out the local flavor of New England character and language. This regional approach, much used by writers in all sections of the country during the post-Civil War years, would seem to owe something to the frontier influence, nothing to Aristotle or Poe. Miss Jewett is more interested in her people and their language than in achieving dramatic movement or effect.

If Miss Jewett has a theme, it is that of indicating the superiority of the old rural Yankee simplicity to the new urban complexity. However, she does not dwell upon the contrast between the old and new, Faulkner fashion, but contents herself with a faithful and loving rendering of her New England landscapes and portraits.

"The Courting of Sister Wisby" is more tall tale than story. A narrator with a keen eye for details of nature and character takes a walk through the New England backwoods and gets into conversation with "dear old Mrs. Goodsoe, the friend of my childhood and fond dependence of my maturer years." As in "The Celebrated Jumping Frog," the second narrator takes over and tells the central story in the vernacular. Mrs. Goodsoe rambles along, talking about herbs and the art of healing, and only incidentally comes to Miss Wisby late in the story. Poe would not approve. However, the story has life and freshness and humor. Miss Wisby, a high-strung spinster, takes in a roving preacher during a protracted church meeting, and the courting begins. Despite the eccentricity of the two people, both are practical and decide "to take one another on trial a spell." The preacher runs away once, crying "hang her, let her carry less sail," but somehow they make up and get "married right off fair an' square." Thus the story becomes a lesson in the give and take of marriage. Mrs. Goodsoe guesses that "they got along well as most folks."

In the last quarter of the nineteenth century, naturalism, sometimes called scientific realism, began to influence American literature. Unlike the frontier, which of necessity expressed its influence only in the New World, naturalism was international in scope. Primarily, as developed by Emile Zola and his followers in Europe and America, it was an attempt to give fictional representation to deterministic theories that were developing in biology, philosophy, psychology, and the social sciences. However, since its practitioners were not themselves scientists, it came to include a variety of somewhat contradictory though related elements.

At one extreme naturalist writers sought to give a scientific report on man and the world he lives in, without any thought to pleading a special case. In other words, they sought to develop a pure documentary technique, using words that did no more than denote facts. This approach would seem to place the naturalist outside aesthetic literature, since it denied him the use of his creative resources, particularly the imagination, and made him less important than his materials. Actually there have been very few such literary naturalists. The great "slice of life" stories have always been directed toward the achievement of an effect.

At the opposite extreme naturalists have been special pleaders against social injustice. This approach would also seem to be anti-aesthetic, since it makes of the story a propaganda device rather than a means to the aesthetic enlargement that Poe and James stressed or to the revelation of the complexities of the human personality that concerned Hawthorne and Melville. However, some naturalists became very aesthetic in suggesting, rather than preaching, the needed social cure.

Most naturalists sought in their stories to show that man is not merely influenced by environmental or hereditary forces but is determined by them. This attitude also went against the grain of traditional writers, since it means that man's character has nothing to do with his destiny. His will loses importance and he ceases to have heroic or tragic possibilities. Moreover, heavy-handed efforts to demonstrate this thesis have resulted in inferior stories from the time of Frank Norris to the present. But, again, some naturalists have been very skillful in suggesting rather than stating their deterministic theses. Such naturalists may use the same techniques as non-naturalists; it is only in the effects aimed at that they differ.

Naturalists often took the view that only cultures dominated by the Industrial Revolution, as was America after the Civil War, controlled people in adverse ways. Frontier America, in contrast, stimulated freedom and spontaneity. The effect of the Industrial Revolution was to make the objective world overwhelmingly repressive and to crowd man's subjective life into ever narrower limits. In short, modern man lives in a naturalistic world. In a way these naturalists looked back to the Romantic movement, with its animus against organized society. However, influenced by their un-Romantic conviction of man's helplessness, they encouraged a Utopian improvement of society rather than the assertion of the individual against it.

Naturalism opened up new materials and new techniques for exploration in fiction. Wherever the social scientist went, wherever the psychologist went, the naturalist writer went too. Not only were documentary enumeration and the slice-of-life technique fostered by it, but also the interior monologue, impressionism, expressionism, and even symbolism. As a result, almost all contemporary writers, even those most antinaturalistic in attitude, like Faulkner, owe something to the naturalistic influence.

One of the first American writers to take a tentative step toward naturalism was Hamlin Garland (1860–1940), who knew from experience the hardships of midwestern farmers after the Civil War. Garland called himself a *veritist*, a realist who pushes deeper toward truth than the ordinary realist. In a way he was simply a local colorist, showing the plight of his midwesterners and making a grass-roots protest against economic injustice. But it was a local color that had significance beyond his own region and time. Since Garland America has produced a succession of writers who have developed the theme of social protest, most notably during the Depression — writers like Erskine Caldwell, James T. Farrell, Nelson Algren, and Albert Maltz.

In "The Return of a Private" Garland examines the problems faced by a Civil War soldier as he comes back to his Wisconsin farm. What comes out is not the individuality of this soldier, as in the farm people depicted by Sarah Orne Jewett, but the circumstances that destroy his means to become an individual. A man of "terrible energy" before the war, he returns, weakened by sickness and wounds, to try to restore productivity to a farm that has run down during his absence, to try to give needed food and clothing to his family, to try to regain his own health. Worst of all, he must contend with a "mortgage standing ready with open jaw to swallow half his earnings." Garland indicates that the veteran's plight is typical by naming him "Smith" and by having him return home with two other veterans facing similar problems. In fact, in the final paragraph of the story Garland editorializes: "The common soldier . . . had returned. His war . . . with Nature and against the injustice of his fellow-men was begun again."

This story is weak aesthetically in that it achieves its theme didactically rather than through suggestion. It falls short of naturalism in that the soldier is not so much a victim of an economic system as of injustice. He is viewed as morally good, his fellow-men as morally bad. A more searching naturalist would examine the environment that has produced the fellow-men.

Frank Norris (1870–1902), a disciple of Zola, tried to be such a naturalist. In "A Deal in Wheat" he shows the mechanism of the Chicago grain market, how the maneuvering for position of two capitalists first pushes the price of wheat down to 62 cents a bushel, then up to $2.00 a bushel. Norris also shows the consequences for Sam Lewiston, a farmer. Lewiston is first forced to sell his ranch, then to move to Chicago and become an itinerant worker. Eventually he winds up in a bread line, but when the price of wheat goes to $2.00 a bushel the free distribution of bread is discontinued. Like Garland, Norris makes his point editorially: "The farmer — he who raised the wheat — was ruined upon the one hand; the working man — he who consumed it — was ruined upon the other." However, unlike Garland, Norris is not so interested in attacking the immorality of the two big operators as in indicting the system that permits them to gamble in the lives of people.

Norris's story is no more effective aesthetically than Garland's.

The theme is stated rather than suggested, the action sketched rather than dramatized. The characters are barely outlined. All that one knows about the big operators is that they enjoy the game they are playing, all that one knows about Lewiston is that he is an average human being who wants to work and doesn't relish being kicked around by economic forces.

Theodore Dreiser (1871–1945), one of the chief American theorizers of naturalism, believed that man's chemistry determines his actions and that a kind of social chemistry operates in society. To him Norris's story would simply be analogous to a report of the findings from an experiment in an economics laboratory. In a story called "Typhoon" Dreiser takes us into the social laboratory. The human being to be examined is Ida Zobel, who happens to be physically attractive but has been brought up by strict German immigrant parents. A young man conditioned by society to accept the double standard for men and women easily seduces her, then refuses to take responsibility when she becomes pregnant. She kills him and she and her family are ruined.

Dreiser's story has a kind of enumerative fullness that Norris's lacks, but Dreiser is attempting to do basically the same thing: to show that Ida's destiny is determined by the social system, not by Ida's character. Ida herself never asks if she has done wrong. She is simply concerned with her predicament and is striving helplessly to get out of it.

Inevitably some writers under the influence of naturalism became more interested in their characters or in achieving their naturalistic thesis with aesthetic effect than in the thesis itself. Dreiser himself becomes absorbed in his characters at times, as in "The Lost Phoebe." In this story a midwestern farm couple have achieved a kind of osmosis through years of living together. The wife dies and the husband begins to suffer hallucinations. He pursues his "lost Phoebe" over the countryside. The reader senses

Dreiser's compassion for the old couple and is moved by
derness of the love story and does not concern himself
naturalist's contention that the love and tenderness and
are simply rooted in the chemistry of the physical rela
between man and wife.

One of the finest stories to come out of the naturalist mo
"Paul's Case," was by a writer whose work for the most
not naturalistic. Willa Cather (1876–1947) draws the por
a high school boy who likes to wear a red carnation in his
hole but who lives in a dull, morally narrow Pittsburgh ne
hood. The result of the clash between red carnation tempe
and respectable environment is that Paul first loses out at
and then, being put to work, steals several thousand dollar
his employer and takes off for the red carnation world of New
When dull reality closes in on him again, he plunges ben
train and drops "back into the immense design of things.
gets the impression that Miss Cather, like Dreiser's chemist,
ing certain ingredients and watching the inevitable explosi
character in the story can effectively ask what is wrong with
self and change himself or the world. In fact, no one is expec
— not Paul, who lies and steals, not his father, whose lack of
ination is conditioned by his environment.

Miss Cather, like Dreiser, brings in much external detail t
her story objective reality. It has the appearance of being
mented. But she does more than document; details creep in th
extremely suggestive (Paul's red carnation, for example).
primary concern in fact is for aesthetic effect. The slow, inevi
movement toward the climax and the interplay of balar
themes or motifs suggest the building of a symphony. The
losophy behind the story may be deterministic, but the pres
tion is that of an artist.

Perhaps the best example of a writer developing natural

themes yet working creatively with his materials is Sherwood Anderson (1876–1941). Actually Anderson was not a man to be bound by theories. He was influenced by naturalism because it was in the air he breathed, but there was also a good deal of the romantic in him. Above all, he valued his freedom to follow his creative impulses wherever they led him. He even spoke of writing by feel rather than by plan. "The short story," he once said, "is the result of a sudden passion."

In some of his stories Anderson seems to be following in the wake of Mark Twain — in language, in technique, and in theme. In "I'm a Fool" a boy, speaking the language of Huck Finn, naively exposes the lying that goes on in small-town America, little realizing that his own lying, like Huck's, has grown out of the community lying. Thus the technique is that of irony and the theme has to do with American failure. The failure, Anderson is suggesting (not telling us), is that America doesn't provide the boy with a milieu in which his spontaneous goodness can find expression. But Anderson is not so much appealing through his theme for social change as he is poignantly suggesting the contrast between ideal and actuality. The success of the story stems from his capturing of the boy's language and from the subtlety of the presentation of the theme.

The heroes of Anderson's more naturalistic stories are yearners after experience smothered in a world that demands conformity. Like Chekhov, who influenced him, Anderson treats them with great sympathy and compassion. Often, as with Chekhov, what goes on inside his characters, their hidden life, is more important than what occurs on the surface. Influenced by psychoanalysis, he works with interior monologues to bring out this inner life. In the end his naturalism probes so deeply that it disappears into mystery. Science, instead of clarifying all, itself becomes antinaturalistic.

The characters in these more naturalistic stories tend to become

grotesques because of the distorted expression that their yearning takes. The naturalistic influence is obvious: they seem to be working out their compulsions, not wrestling with their consciences. But the motivations behind their compulsions are so complex that the naturalism suggests no solutions, only leaves the reader yearning himself. In "Unlighted Lamps" a daughter sees herself in relation to the tangled lives of her mother and father, and to the dark undergrowth of the community. Both she and the father seek to extricate themselves by groping toward the light of love, but the lamps are unlighted and Anderson leaves the father dead and the daughter helpless. He seems to be brooding over the story, experiencing his own feeling of helplessness about their tangled misshapen lives. As in "I'm a Fool," there is the Chekhovian longing for life as it might be but an acceptance of life as it is. One also feels the influence of Freud, and there are strong Gothic overtones both in the exterior scenes and in the interior views of daughter and father.

Another writer who probes the interior of his characters, searching like a scientist for their diseases, is William Carlos Williams (1883–   ), who as a New Jersey doctor has had much opportunity to observe American life. In "The Use of Force" a doctor forces open the mouth of a neurotic child and discovers that she has diphtheria. But the doctor's terse notes reveal him to be less concerned with the child's physical disease than with the disease that the use of force ironically uncovers in himself. His disease may be viewed naturalistically as Freudian or spiritually as original sin; Williams leaves the matter open. He does suggest that the doctor's insight, however interpreted, will help him to meet future crises.

John Steinbeck (1902–   ) throws man's lot back on the environment. He believes in spiritual life but sees it as distorted or stunted except under friendly conditions. In "The Leader of the

People" the grandfather looks back with longing to an epic period in American development, the period of the conquest of the frontier. Then he was a "leader of the people." The father, in contrast, is a product of our contemporary machine-dominated culture and lacks sympathy for the grandfather. He also is a smaller man spiritually. Hence Steinbeck seems to connect the spiritual element in both men to environment. Ultimately environment controls; a noble spirit does not express itself unless environment permits. Steinbeck would seem to be appealing for the building of a more perfect environment in the future.

The hard facts of naturalism challenged some writers to discover the spiritual resources of their characters. To them naturalism simply shifted the emphasis from the old facts of life that man had always faced — death, pain, catastrophe, madness, evil — to the social environment. Society became the new enemy to be transcended. These writers looked back toward the spiritually triumphant hero of the past and forward toward the existentialist hero of the present. They helped provide the milieu from which existentialist philosophy and literature could spring.

Stephen Crane (1871–1900) was strongly influenced by naturalism, both in his respect for environment as a controlling force and in his respect for detail observed from life. Yet he develops a spiritual element that transcends environment, and technically he achieves a suggestiveness that refuses to subordinate itself to the surface meaning of words.

In "The Open Boat" Crane pictures four men physically small in their battle for survival against the ocean. To them the ocean is not animated by hostile gods, as with the ancient Greeks, but is simply a manifestation of a nature indifferent to their fate. But they themselves have subjective resources that they throw into the battle. They have courage and they have awareness of a "subtle brotherhood of men." They are not victims. Their spiritual enlargement shows most fully in the oiler. The strongest of the four, he might have saved himself had he been motivated by the principle of survival by "tooth and claw." Instead he leaves the injured captain the boat to hang onto and the cook the life belt, and strikes out on his own and dies. The reader mourns his death because he has spiritually enlisted the reader's sympathies. Crane is recognizing the strength of the forces that destroy man but indicating that man must seek to conquer them, even though he can never achieve more than a partial victory.

In "The Blue Hotel" Crane carefully sets up the social forces that contribute to a killing, then has the men who express the social forces imply their own responsibility. The victim, the Swede, comes into the American West with a stereotyped conception of the region. The people he meets laugh at him at first, then gradually take over their expected roles, and the Swede winds up dead in a barroom. Social processes working themselves out, says the reader; no one is responsible, no one could have acted differently. But Crane does not stop at this point. The men involved in the action are disturbed, uncertain. The easterner of the story finally says, "I refused to stand up and be a man. I let the Swede fight it out alone. . . . We, five of us, have collaborated in the murder of this Swede." And the final comment in the story, that by the cowboy, is a partial confession: "Well, I didn't do anythin', did I?"

Crane approaches the technique of writing in the same spirit. He dares to experiment — to work boldly with impressionism, symbolism, and irony. At his best he is not content simply to give verisimilitude to a scene. The captain, clinging to the keel of the overturned boat, "appeared like a man raising himself to look over a board fence, if it were not for the extraordinary gymnastics of the boat." Here the reader gets the impression of the scene; the few details are suggestive beyond themselves. Sometimes Crane uses color to achieve the impressionistic effect, as, for example, the blue hotel that screams and howls against the dazzling winter landscape. Crane's symbolism is equally bold. In "The Open Boat" the tower on the beach symbolizes a god indifferent to man: "This tower was a giant, standing with its back to the plight of the ants." Crane brings irony into play with the death of the oiler, the strongest of the four men, and in the central effect of "The Blue Hotel," the destruction of the Swede by a force that he projects from his own mind into the world.

Ernest Hemingway (1898–1961), who acknowledged Crane as one of his American influences, has Crane's zest for testing man's spiritual existence against the trapping forces and also his great interest in technique. Thematically, Hemingway's stories either give an uninitiated character illumination into the forces, or show a character battling the forces in such a way as to gain dignity. The first sort of story is really a preparation for the second. Given education into reality, a person can then take his measures to deal with it. These stories become a handbook for existentialism, since they throw responsibility upon the individual, not, as with the naturalists, upon the trapping forces.

A story of the first kind is "Indian Camp" (Nick Adams discovers the harsh existence of death, then tries to build up his defenses anew), a story of the second kind, "The Snows of Kilimanjaro" (Harry discovers his own moral corruption and that of the world he has let influence him and, on his deathbed, tries to make a moral comeback).

Hemingway's achievement lies in the manner in which he renders his themes: through a language that is a kind of fusion of Huck Finn and Gertrude Stein; through sensory detail that brings the physical world to the reader with lyrical freshness or excruciating horror (Hemingway once said that his greatest problem in writing "was to put down what really happened in action; what

the actual things were which produced the emotion that you ex-
perienced"); through symbols embedded in the natural world (the
bones of the leopard high on the mountain side in "The Snows of
Kilimanjaro"); through a dialogue that is as suggestive as his sensory detail; through the slow building of his dramatic fires toward
an explosive flame.

"Indian Camp" brings out many of Hemingway's qualities. At
the beginning of the story Nick Adams is rowing across a lake to
watch his father, a doctor, bring life into the world. This he sees —
not childbirth as he would like to believe that it happens, but as
it really happens. He also sees something more, the suicide death
of the Indian father, who cannot stand the pain of the mother.
The story hinges, then, on Aristotle's key structural elements, recognition and irony. More than this, Hemingway, the master, brings
home the recognition and the irony, the emotion that Nick experiences, by the concreteness with which he puts down "the actual
things." First there is the fresh immediacy of the ride across the
lake ("Nick heard the oar-locks of the other boat quite a way ahead
of them in the mist"); second, the reality of childbirth ("Later
when he started to operate Uncle George and three Indian men
held the woman still"); third, the unrelenting specification of the
father's death ("The blood had flowed down into a pool where
his body sagged the bunk"); and finally the freshness of nature
once more as Nick seeks to regain his balance ("Nick trailed his
hand in the water. It felt warm in the sharp chill of the morning").
This last touch, the hand warm in the water, shows the symbolist
in Hemingway working. Nick is looking for the reassertion of life.
He "felt quite sure that he would never die."

F. Scott Fitzgerald (1896–1940), who divided his efforts between
serious and popular writing, lacks Hemingway's definiteness of
purpose but at his best outdistances Hemingway in the complexity with which he probes the human heart. A torn personality him-

self, Fitzgerald found nothing about life simple. In "The Rich Boy" he endlessly analyzes Anson Hunter and the rich world in which Anson functions, yet never arrives at a conclusive answer to whether Anson is a naturalistic victim of his wealth or a moral failure. He poses the problem, leaving us both sorry for Anson and critical of him. His reluctance to condemn Anson contrasts sharply with Hemingway's unswerving moral rejection of the rich wife in "The Snows of Kilimanjaro." Yet there is a gain for Fitzgerald in the depth of his study and in his compassion, as against the one-sidedness and coldness of Hemingway's portrayal.

William Faulkner (1897–   ) is the most important figure in a southern upsurge in literature that began after World War I. Whereas Hemingway usually sees the environment, whatever its nature, as hostile to the individual, as something to be combated, the southern writers single out the materialistic modern world as the chief offender and look back to the traditional societies of the past for environments favorable to the dignity of man. In particular they distrust the forces released by the great scientific revolutions of the past four hundred years. Faulkner, for example, divides his characters into several categories: naturalistic characters who permit the forces to do with their lives as they will (Flem Snopes, Jason Compson); characters who succumb to the forces with a sense of their own moral failure (Caddy Compson and her father); characters who wage a desperate, losing battle against the forces (Quentin Compson, Miss Emily Grierson); characters who triumph morally, who endure (Ike McCaslin, Dilsey). Faulkner shows compassion for all except those in the first category.

Faulkner operates within the context of a disintegrating South, a world in transition from a culture partly at odds with naturalistic forces to one that embraces the forces. In "A Rose for Emily" he pictures Miss Emily living behind barricaded doors, protecting herself from a hostile world. She has become a tiny island of the past surrounded by the ocean of the present. Whenever the present laps too high, she hurls back the waves. Hence "a rose for Emily," an accolade for her. But she wins her victory at too great cost — she is a distorted personality.

The story is in the Gothic horror tradition, but rooted in reality. Growing up in the aftermath of the Civil War, Miss Emily has led a tortured life. Her father dominates her, keeping the young men away from her — presumably because the eligible bachelors have been killed off in the war. After his death she asserts her own will by taking up with a Yankee construction foreman, Homer Barron. Then when Homer proves to be a "naturalistic" man, a hollow man, she keeps him faithful by killing him. That is, the dead Homer continues to share her bed, as the townspeople discover many years later when she herself dies.

Faulkner's language in this story, as in others, looks back to Twain and to southern oratorical rhetoricians. Faulkner has Twain's fine ear for the vernacular, for the language of southern whites and Negroes. He also has Twain's broad vernacular humor, though this characteristic is brought out better in a story like "Spotted Horses" than in "A Rose for Emily." Faulkner's rhetorical outbursts sometimes rise from the seething consciousnesses of his characters, giving his experiments in expressionism a flavor peculiar to him. At times his rhetoric gets out of hand, but it is never more carefully controlled than in "Miss Emily"; for example, in the tableau of the old men of the town near the end of the story. This tableau also brings out Faulkner's talent for painting a picture, as does the initial portrait of Miss Emily. "She looked bloated, like a body long submerged in motionless water, and of that pallid hue. Her eyes, lost in the fatty ridges of her face, looked like two small pieces of coal pressed into a lump of dough as they moved from one face to another . . ."

Katherine Anne Porter (1894–   ) and Caroline Gordon

(1895–   ) are preoccupied with the same traditional values as Faulkner, but their technique is more polished than his, more in the manner of Henry James, less in that of the western writers. Still another writer associated with the southern literary renaissance is Robert Penn Warren (1905–   ). In "When the Light Turns Green," he seems closer to Sherwood Anderson than to Faulkner in the way that he develops a boy's point of view and language. However, the boy is not, like Anderson's boy, discovering the corruption of the only world he knows but witnessing the passing of a traditional world, his grandfather's, and the rise of a materialistic world, that of the "sons-of-bitches" in town. In "Old Mortality" Miss Porter is raising this question: Where is the new southern generation that has lost faith in the values of the past headed? Miranda, the sensitive spokesman for the new generation, has confidence in the superiority of her generation. But Miss Porter suggests that she is simply lost in the big world, without any values. She has still to discover her awful freedom and aloneness.

In "Old Red" Miss Gordon shows a different sort of rebel, Mr. Maury. He has engaged in a long-drawn-out struggle against the conventional morality of his wife, now dead, and her family. Coming to the end of his years, he is searching for the meaning in this struggle, to see where the issue lies. And as he struggles, images from the past flash before him and mingle with those from the present. He becomes Old Red, the fox of his youth who could not be hunted into a corner. He has asserted the immortality of the aesthetic life, a life that will never be completely trapped, that will raise its head in the most impossible of situations. Miss Gordon is aesthetically daring in the handling of the flashbacks, in her use of the symbol of the fox, and in her final subjective merging of Mr. Maury and the fox.

Another way that writers have taken to throw moral responsibility back upon man has been through satire. They rub man's face in his smallness, ridiculing him for not rising to his possibilities. Sometimes the satire is spoofing, as in stories like "The Secret Life of Walter Mitty" and "The Catbird Seat" by James Thurber. Sometimes it is caustic, as in the stories of Ring Lardner.

On the surface Lardner (1885–1933), a midwestern sports writer to begin with, seems almost naturalistic. By the time he gets through submerging a character in his narrow American milieu, one may well wonder what chance the character has to assert freedom of will. Yet Lardner is showing, with the bitter humor of a Swift, man's shortcomings. He wants his Americans to see that they have moral choice but that in their mean-spiritedness they close their eyes to it.

In his language Lardner follows the western tradition of Twain, writing in the vernacular of ignorant, semiliterate people. He gets some of his humorous effects through malapropisms and achieves his satire through exposing the appalling lack of insight of his characters. In "The Golden Honeymoon" the husband, using ludicrously bad grammar, recollects the "wonderful" trip he and his wife took to Florida in celebration of their golden anniversary. Both reveal themselves concerned only with self-interest, with cruelty at others' expense, with triteness, with absorption in meaningless details, with sentimentality. The climax comes when the honeymooners, after quarreling endlessly, decide to put up a front. " 'Listen, Charley,' she said. 'This is our Golden Honeymoon and we don't want the whole thing spoilt with a silly old quarrel.' " After that "I put my arm around her shoulder and she stroked my hand and I guess we got kind of spoony."

"Big Blonde," by Dorothy Parker (1893–   ), seems to verge on naturalism and yet to be something different. It also seems to verge on Lardner's satire and yet to be different from that, too. The tone of Miss Parker's language is that of Lardner, though tempered by the use of the third-person point of view. She presents much the same starved, arid social milieu. It is the prohibition era in New York and the big blonde, Hazel Morse, is a model caught up in a world of drinking and eating and love-making. It is a world in which popularity is important, and Hazel prides herself on being a good sport. But just as her feet are pinched by her high-heeled slippers, so her personality is pinched by trying to be happy all the time. Yet when she gives in to uncheerful moods, she loses popularity and people leave her. All through the story people are either leaving her or counseling her to buck up and be happy.

The naturalistic element in the story is expressed through the pervasiveness of the social desert in which the characters live. They can no more escape it than they can escape the air they breathe. Nevertheless Miss Parker does seem to hold them responsible. She does so by showing Hazel, dumb as she is, groping to lift herself from the morass. And she does so with wonderful, ludicrous irony, and also with pathos. Indeed there is an affirmation of human dignity not to be found in Lardner's story.

One mark of the writing of the twentieth century is the sheer volume of good stories. More have been published in America than during the entire preceding history of American and English letters. Moreover, so many writers have written at least several superior stories that it is difficult to list them, much less comment on them. A partial list would include, aside from the writers discussed in this pamphlet, Conrad Aiken, James T. Farrell, Stephen Vincent Benét, John O'Hara, Thomas Wolfe, Ellen Glasgow, Ruth Suckow, Glenway Wescott, John Cheever, William March, Truman Capote, Jesse Stuart, Mary McCarthy, Carson McCullers, William Saroyan, Jerome Weidman, Sally Benson, Kay Boyle, Irwin Shaw, Jean Stafford, Walter Van Tilburg Clark, J. D.

Salinger, Andrew Lytle, Thomas Mabry, Hortense Calisher, John Updike, Philip Roth, Peter Taylor, and Flannery O'Connor.

Experimentation with technique is another mark of the writing of our time. Hemingway, with his development of a style that explodes the reader into the story, Faulkner with his use of a stream of consciousness that manhandles time, language, and cause and effect, Caroline Gordon with her flashbacks within flashbacks, are symptomatic of what has been going on. Similar experimentation has occurred in the other arts. The big problem apparently has been to bring man's chaotic subconscious life into the ordered world of the artist. Neither the external nor the internal world is as neatly outlined as it once was for him.

Other than Faulkner the southerner most given to experimentation with technique is Eudora Welty (1909–   ). In most good stories a problem is introduced in the opening paragraph, and the forward movement of the story depends upon its development and solution. But in "Powerhouse" the reader has to search hard for a problem for the main character to overcome. In the opening scene we see Powerhouse and his Negro jazz band playing at a white dance in a Mississippi town. During the pauses in the music Powerhouse improvises a story about the death of his wife in New York. Later, during intermission, he elaborates upon the story at a Negro café and finally admits it to be untrue. In the concluding scene the orchestra returns to its playing at the dance. The reader delights in Miss Welty's rendering of Powerhouse's vitality and warmth, in the pagan innocence and grace of the Negroes, and in the lyrical spontaneity of the language. And yet he wonders where the story lies.

Actually Miss Welty is developing her story in the pattern of a symphony. She sets up a series of motifs and then elaborates on them and eventually achieves a climax. Powerhouse, as piano player and orchestra leader, is introduced as an improviser. He

41

does not follow a score, he creates a new piece of music each time he plays it. He also encompasses the other musicians in his personality, yet depends upon them. At one extreme is Little Brother, the clarinetist, at the other, Scoot the drummer. In the middle is Valentine, the bass fiddler. Powerhouse pleads with Valentine to go higher and looks to Scoot for direction when he himself seems lost.

Next we see the theme of each musician reappear as Powerhouse tells his story about his wife. Again Powerhouse is the improviser, now leading his men on, now getting his cue from them. Little Brother is most gullible; he believes anything Powerhouse tells him. Scoot, on the other hand, is disbelieving, keeping Powerhouse from soaring too high. In the café scene a waitress introduces a new motif; the game goes on, Powerhouse's orchestra never stops playing. By the end of the story we realize that we have participated in a pagan love song, a love song to Powerhouse's wife, and that the song raises questions and answers them. What is to keep Gypsy faithful while Powerhouse is away from home? How are the dark forces of life to be met? These are the questions. And the answer: She is to be kept faithful through a kind of knocking on wood — through the reliving of one's fears in fantasy, through a continuous immersion in the fresh waters of creation.

The most successful satirist of post-World War II America is J. F. Powers (1917–   ). A Catholic, Powers examines the role of the Church in the upper Midwest. Does the Church live by accommodating itself to worldly pressure or by defying it? This is "the overwhelming question" that Powers poses in his stories. Father Urban, a priest appearing in several of them, continually blinds himself to the extent of his accommodation, but when pushed to extremes takes a spiritual stand. The worldly tempter is Billy Cosgrove, Father Urban's rich patron. In "God Writes a Bad Hand" Billy takes Father Urban on a fishing trip, and Father Urban is made increasingly aware that Billy's patronage is only a bribe, that Billy is complacently unaware of Christian love. Father Urban wrestles with his conscience but does nothing to combat Billy except to appear a bit disgruntled. Even slight disgruntlement is too much for Billy; he must have a complete victory. While fishing they encounter a deer in a lake, and Billy overtakes it and shoves its head under water. Only then does Father Urban take his stand, and after an agonizing moment of indecision. When he guns the motor, Billy loses his grip and the deer is saved.

Powers seems to say in this story that if enough pressure is put on the Church, it comes alive. However, he is not sanguine as to the depths of the rebirth. Thus at the end of the story, Father Urban is relieved to discover that Billy's abandonment of him is only partial. "All is not lost." Powers's satire is less biting than Lardner's. He is less angry at evil, perhaps has a deeper understanding of it.

The Beat Generation writers rebel against the world that Powers criticizes. They see a "square" America full of "other-directed" people seeking to accommodate themselves to the technological process, to the Billy Cosgroves who run things, to organizations. They scorn the reluctant and partial resistances of people like Father Urban. They feel that nothing short of shock treatment will arouse America to a more vital approach to life. They worship at the shrine of sensation, of sensation that will explode into a great, enlarging experience. They run from order, they welcome chaos. Drink, sex, dope, wild driving, frenzied music — anything goes that will bring the explosion.

In "Fracture" R. V. Cassill (1919–   ) shows a husband caught in the middle between his "square" wife and a "beat" friend. The wife Margaret stands for order, cleanliness, and respectability. The friend Harold follows every whim and leads a disorderly chaotic life. He is continually irritating Margaret, and Worth, the hus-

43

band, agrees to give up Harold. "Hon, it's all settled. Goodbye to Harold." But Harold, despite his nihilism, is somehow alive, while Margaret's existence is utterly sterile. And in the end Worth envies Harold — "his enemies, his dirty room, his mammoth drunks, his cough, his Sarah."

It has been theorized that the Beat, in casting his lot with Dionysus and completely rejecting Apollo, is expressing a psychopathic reaction to the Atomic Age and the concentration camps. Confronted with atomic power, with an overwhelmingly naturalistic world, man feels helpless and, in a frenzied outburst of protest, releases all his impulses. He makes the ultimate romantic rebellion against the conditions of his life. Jack Kerouac (1922–   ), who gave the Beat movement its name, seems to voice this theory in "The Time of the Geek." Leon Levinsky, the poet of the story, explains the meaning of the Nickel-O, an amusement place frequented by "old drunks, whores, queers, all kinds of characters, hoods, junkies, all the castoffs of bourgeois society." The Nickel-O, Levinsky says, is a symbol: "it's the place where the atomic disease was first noticed and from which it will spread, slowly and insiduously . . ."

The Beats carry their rebellion into their manner of writing. They feel that the followers of Aristotle and Poe and James have lost vitality. They have little use for a story that builds toward effect or recognition. They scorn technical triumphs of the artist. Their own stories tend to zigzag madly, reaching for moments of ecstasy, achieving them, and then plunging off in a new direction. They feel that they have gained life even if they have lost form.

As of the present moment, it is hard to say where the American short story will go next. The Beat Generation is quite right in seeing that the problem is one of vitality. This is always the basic problem. But if the experimenters in technique seem to be running into a wall, so do the Beats. They have made their point, and now they are repeating it. They reach the West Coast, and then they turn back. Lacking form, their stories, once the newness has worn off, are all the duller for the repetition and the failure in technique.

But even if we don't know where the American short story is going next, we can see from the writers and stories we have examined that it has established a strong and varied life. It has done so in every way imaginable — in presentation of the full range of American experience, in exploration of vital and universal themes, in experimentation with technique and style, in search for language. It has both kept pace with literary development in the rest of the world and maintained its own American character. Even now we can feel it, like Whitman's spider, launching forth "filament, filament, filament, out of itself,/ Ever unreeling them, ever tirelessly speeding them."

↙ *Selected Bibliography*

Collections of American Short Stories

The Best American Short Stories. Boston: Houghton Mifflin. (Annual publication, currently edited by Martha Foley and David Burnett.)

Brooks, Cleanth, and Robert Penn Warren, eds. *An Anthology of Stories from the Southern Review*. Baton Rouge: Louisiana State University Press, 1953.

Brown, Leonard, ed. *Modern American and British Short Stories*. New York: Harcourt, Brace, 1929.

Burrell, Angus, and Bennett Cerf, eds. *An Anthology of Famous American Short Stories*. New York: Random House, 1953.

Current-Garcia, Eugene, and Walton R. Patrick, eds. *American Short Stories: 1820 to the Present*. Chicago: Scott, Foresman, 1952.

Feldman, Gene, and Max Gartenberg, eds. *The Beat Generation and the Angry Young Men*. New York: Dell, 1958.

Gold, Herbert, and David L. Stevenson, eds. *Stories of Modern America*. New York: St. Martin's Press, 1961.

Hibbard, Addison, ed. *Stories of the South: Old and New*. Chapel Hill: University of North Carolina Press, 1931.

Jessup, Alexander, ed. *Representative American Short Stories*. New York: Macmillan, 1944.

Ludwig, Jack Barry, and W. Richard Poirier, eds. *Stories: British and American*. Boston: Houghton Mifflin, 1953.

The O. Henry Award Prize Stories. New York: Doubleday. (Annual publication, currently edited by Mary Stegner.)

Pattee, Fred Lewis, ed. *Century Readings in the American Short Story*. New York: D. Appleton-Century, 1927.

Prescott, Orville, ed. *Mid-Century: An Anthology of Distinguished Contemporary American Short Stories*. New York: Pocket Books, 1958.

Ramsey, Robert, ed. *Short Stories of America*. Boston: Houghton Mifflin, 1921.

Short Stories from the New Yorker. New York: Simon and Schuster, 1940. (Also *55 Short Stories from the New Yorker*, 1949; and *Stories from the New Yorker*, 1960.)

Stegner, Wallace and Mary, eds. *Great American Short Stories*. New York: Dell, 1957.

Stern, Philip Van Doren, ed. *The Pocket Book of Modern American Short Stories*. New York: Pocket Books, 1954.

Taggard, Ernestine, ed. *Twenty Grand Short Stories*. New York: Bantam, 195-?

West, Ray B., Jr., ed. *American Short Stories*. New York: Thomas Y. Crowell, 1959.

Theoretical Works on the Short Story

Aldridge, John, ed. *Critiques and Essays on Modern Fiction*. New York: Ronald Press, 1952.

Bates, H. E. *The Modern Short Story*. London, New York: Nelson, 1941.

Bement, Douglas, and Ross M. Taylor. *The Fabric of Fiction*. New York: Harcourt, Brace, 1948.

Blair, Walter. *Native American Humor (1800–1900)*. New York: American Book, 1937.

Brooks, Cleanth, Jr., and Robert Penn Warren, eds. *Understanding Fiction*. New York: Appleton-Century-Crofts, 1953.

Current-Garcia, Eugene, and Walton R. Patrick. *What Is the Short Story?* Chicago: Scott, Foresman, 1961.

Gordon, Caroline, and Allen Tate, eds. *The House of Fiction: An Anthology of the Short Story with Commentary*. New York: Scribner's, 1950.

James, Henry. *The Art of Fiction and Other Essays*. New York: Oxford University Press, 1948.

Matthews, Brander. *The Philosophy of the Short Story*. New York: Longmans, Green, 1901.

O'Brien, Edward J. *The Advance of the American Short Story*. New York: Dodd, Mead, 1923.

————. *The Dance of the Machines: The American Short Story and the Industrial Age*. New York: Macaulay, 1929.

O'Connor, William Van, ed. *Forms of Modern Fiction*. Minneapolis: University of Minnesota Press, 1948. Paperback edition, Bloomington: Indiana University Press.

O'Faolain, Sean. *The Short Story*. New York: Devin-Adair, 1951.

Pattee, Fred Lewis. *The Development of the American Short Story: An Historical Survey*. New York: Harper, 1923.

Ward, Alfred C. *Aspects of the Modern Short Story: English and American*. London: University of London Press, 1924.

Welty, Eudora. *Short Stories*. New York: Harcourt, Brace, 1949.

West, Ray B., Jr. *The Short Story in America*. Chicago: Regnery, 1952.

West, Ray B., Jr., and Robert Wooster Stallman, eds. *The Art of Modern Fiction*. New York: Rinehart, 1949.

Wharton, Edith. *The Writing of Fiction*. New York: Scribner's, 1925.

Woolf, Virginia. *Granite and Rainbow*. New York: Harcourt, Brace, 1958.

Little Cottontail

BY CARL MEMLING

PICTURES BY LILIAN OBLIGADO

gb GOLDEN PRESS
Western Publishing Company, Inc.
Racine, Wisconsin

Lilian Obligado was so enchanted with Carl Memling's LITTLE COTTON-
TAIL that she bought herself a rabbit. The two became great friends,
and Miss Obligado's obvious enjoyment of her pet is clearly seen
in these charming pictures. We hope that Little Cottontail will
make many more new friends through this Little Golden Book.

Tenth Printing, 1975

Once there was a little cottontail rabbit who lived in a cozy nest.

"Mother," said the little cottontail, "when will I grow up?"

"Soon," said his mother.

"But first, Little Cottontail, you must leave the nest."

"Leave the nest?" he said.

His little round nest was just the right size. It was soft and warm with a bed made of grass and tufts of fur. It was a nice nest.

A mother and a father robin peered down at him.
Their babies were still too young to leave the nest.
They wondered what Little Cottontail would do.

With a flop and a hop, and a hump and a bump,
Little Cottontail left the nest.

"NOW am I grown up?" he asked.

His mother smiled. "Not yet," she said. "First,
Little Cottontail, you must learn to wash yourself."

"Please teach me," he said.

"Watch closely," said the mother.

A porcupine sitting on a hollow log watched
closely, too.

"This is the way you wash yourself early in the morning.

"Shake your feet, one at a time. Then lick them clean, one at a time.

"Scrub your face with your little front paws.

"Scratch your ears with your big hind paws.

"Then fluff all your fur up, and lick it clean—and you'll be bright and shining early in the morning."
"I can do all that," said Little Cottontail.
And he did.

"Didn't he do that very well!" a deermouse whis-
pered to her tiny children.

"NOW am I grown up?" asked Little Cottontail.

"Not yet," said his mother.

"First, Little Cottontail, you must learn what big rabbits eat . . .

"Out in the meadow all summer long, they eat grass and herbs and lots of green plants.

"Over by the farmhouse all summer long, they eat carrots and cabbage and nice fresh fruit.

"All through the winter, white with snow, they eat buds and twigs and the bark of trees.

"These are things that big rabbits eat whenever they are hungry."

Little Cottontail said, "I listened closely, and I think I know them."

And he did.

"NOW am I grown up?" asked Little Cottontail.

"Not yet!" hissed a woodchuck, popping up from his burrow. "First you must learn about foxes!"

"What about foxes?" said Little Cottontail.

"Foxes like to chase rabbits," said his mother. "They like to catch them for dinner.

"You must learn how to tell that a fox is coming. Please, Little Cottontail, watch very closely...

"This is the way you twitch your nose — *sniff-sniff, sniff-sniff . . . sniff-sniff-sniff* — to sniff the air for the smell of a fox.

"And this is the way you cock your ears, and raise your head, and glance about—to see if that bad fox is coming near.

"And if the fox comes, this is the way you lay back your ears and bound away. This is the way you hop, hop, hop as fast as you can, before the fox can catch you.

"You dodge and you twist and you take short cuts.

"You zigzag and circle and double back on your tracks.

"You lead the fox to a brier patch. You do a quick-quick stop there, and hop to the side. You freeze like a statue—and the fox runs by.

"And all that the fox ever does catch, is a pawful of thorns in the brier patch."

"That's so much to learn," said Little Cottontail.
"Though I did listen closely.

"Now let me see. What came first? . . . Oh, yes.
First I must twitch my nose."

So Little Cottontail twitched his nose to sniff the air for the smell of a fox. Then he cocked his ears and he glanced about . . .

"Mother!" cried Little Cottontail. "A FOX IS COMING!"

Into the hollow log sprang the porcupine. The deermouse scampered off swiftly with her tiny children. Down popped the woodchuck into his burrow. And "Chee chee!" cried the robin as he flew away.

Little Cottontail and his mother laid back their ears and bounded away — and the fox chased after them! "Oh, dear," thought the mother. "What if Little Cottontail doesn't remember all I told him?"

But Little Cottontail zigzagged

and circled

and

doubled back on his tracks.

And then he came to a quick-quick stop and hopped to the side.

He froze like a statue—and the fox ran by, straight into the thorns of a brier patch!

"Mother," said the cottontail, gasping for breath. "NOW am I grown up?"

"Yes," said his mother. "Now you are grown up— BIG COTTONTAIL!"